Concertino
for the Young

Solo with Piano Accompaniment
(*Two copies required for performance*)

Dennis Alexander

Contents

Alfred Music
P.O. Box 10003
Van Nuys, CA 91410-0003
alfred.com

ISBN-10: 1-4706-4183-6
ISBN-13: 978-1-4706-4183-2

Cover art:
Watercolor background: © Getty Images / lutavia • Watercolor grand piano: © iStockphoto / nats77

Dedicated to my friend and musical colleague, Kat Dubinski

Concertino for the Young

I.

Dennis Alexander

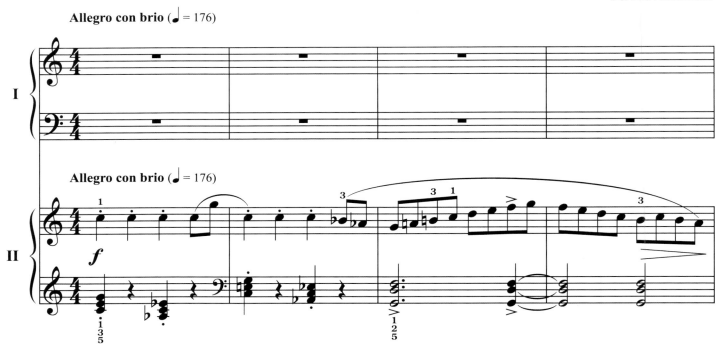

II.

9

III.

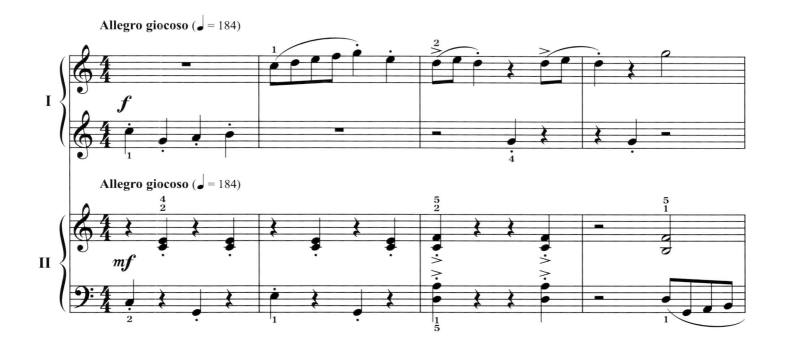